D1486770

RUSSIAN
FOOD AND DRINK

Valentina Lapenkova
and Edward Lambton

The Bookwright Press
New York · 1988

FOOD AND DRINK

Chinese Food and Drink
French Food and Drink
Greek Food and Drink
Indian Food and Drink

Italian Food and Drink
Japanese Food and Drink
Russian Food and Drink
Spanish Food and Drink

First published in the
United States in 1988 by
The Bookwright Press
387 Park Avenue South
New York, NY 10016

First published in 1987 by
Wayland (Publishers) Limited
61 Western Road, Hove
East Sussex BN3 1JD, England

ISBN 0–531–18175–8
Library of Congress Catalog Card Number: 87–71743

Typeset by DP Press, Sevenoaks, Kent
Printed in Italy by G. Canale & C.S.p.A., Turin

Cover   *Tea is a very popular drink in the USSR. The samovar (left) heats the water and keeps the tea hot once it is made.*

Contents

Russia and its people

Russia today is the largest of the 15 constituent republics of the USSR (or Soviet Union), covering three-quarters of its territory. More than half of the population of the USSR are Russians, so it is not surprising to find that "Russia" and "USSR" are often taken to mean the same thing. But within the USSR, the people speak 130 languages and belong to 150 nationalities. The lands they occupy stretch from the Baltic Sea in Eastern Europe, 10,000 km (6,200 mi) eastward to the Bering Strait, which is only 64 km (40 mi) from Alaska.

The USSR was established after the Russian Revolution of 1917, from the lands of the former Russian Empire. Today it is one of the world's two "superpowers," and is governed from Moscow, the ancient capital of Russia.

From the map, you can see that the USSR has land boundaries with twelve other countries. There are

The Kremlin Palace and the Moskva River.

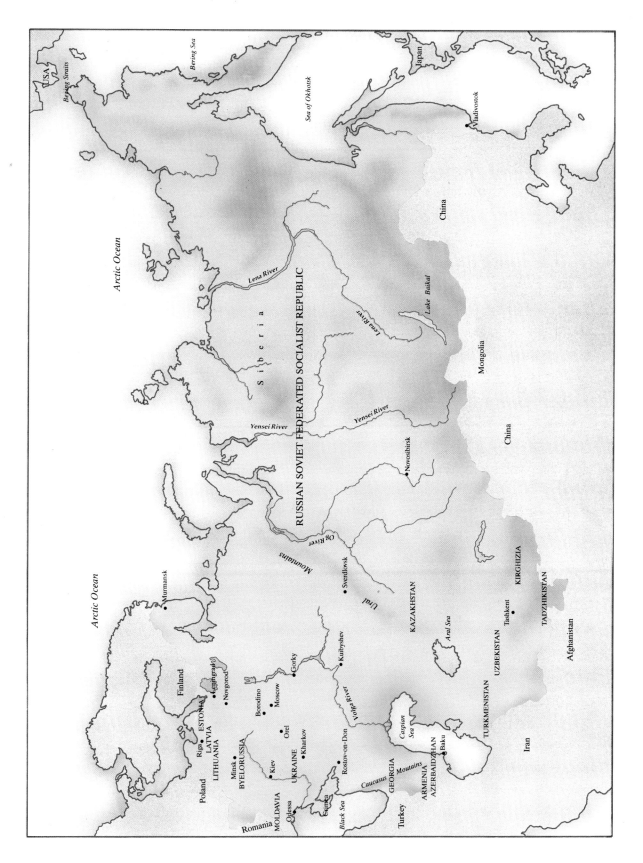

Arctic Ocean

Bering Straits

USA

Bering Sea

Sea of Okhotsk

Japan

Vladivostok

China

Arctic Ocean

Murmansk

Lena River

Lena River

Lake Baikal

S i b e r i a

RUSSIAN SOVIET FEDERATED SOCIALIST REPUBLIC

Mongolia

China

Yensei River

Yensei River

Ob River

Novosibirsk

Ural Mountains

Sverdlovsk

Finland

Leningrad

Novgorod

Gorky

Kuibyshev

KAZAKHSTAN

Aral Sea

KIRGHIZIA

Tashkent

TADZHIKISTAN

UZBEKISTAN

TURKMENISTAN

Afghanistan

Moscow

Borodino

ESTONIA

LATVIA

Riga

LITHUANIA

Minsk

BYELORUSSIA

Kiev

Orel

Kharkov

UKRAINE

Rostov-on-Don

Volga River

Caspian Sea

AZERBAIDZHAN

Baku

Iran

Poland

MOLDAVIA

Odessa

Romania

Crimea

Black Sea

Caucasus Moutains

Turkey

GEORGIA

ARMENIA

5

few natural borders in this great territory to separate one country from another. Even the Ural Mountains, dividing Europe and Asia, are seldom more than 600 m (2,000 ft) high.

The Russians are a Slavic people like the Poles, the Yugoslavians, the Czechs and the Slovaks. They are all descendants of an ancient people who lived in Eastern Europe more than 4,000 years ago. The Slavs were dominated for a long time by adventurous and wandering tribes like the Goths and the Vikings, and harassed by invading nomads — Huns, Mongols, Tartars and Turks — coming from the Steppes of Central Asia. By the middle of the seventh century A.D. there were many Slav cities ruled by princes and trading in furs, wax and honey with Western Europe.

The gleaming spires of Kiev, once one of the most splendid cities in Europe.

The Swedish Vikings colonized the Russian shores of the Baltic Sea during the eighth and ninth centuries. They wanted to develop a trading route to the Greeks, so they gained control of the routes running from the Slav city of Great Novgorod, down through Kiev and the Black Sea, to the ancient port of Constantinople. These Vikings became rulers and protectors of the Slavs, but within 100 years the Slavs absorbed the Viking princes into their own community. The principality of Kiev Rus grew rich and powerful, and its princes established the first Russian state.

In the year A.D. 988, Prince Vladimir of Kiev selected Eastern Orthodox Christianity as the new religion for Kiev Rus. For more than 200 years, Kiev was one of the most impressive cities in Europe.

But between 1223 and 1240, Kiev Rus was destroyed by the Tartar Mongols, led by Batu, one of the grandsons of Ghengis Khan. They burned every city they captured, enslaved one in ten of its people and slaughtered the rest. After that, Russia remained under Mongol control for 250 years. The Russian craftsmen were taken away to the Mongol hordes. For Russia it was the start of a long period of poverty.

Battles with the Tartars, and other wars, continued for many years. Peasants who lived in the areas affected by them tried to move away, to live in safer places. Laws were passed to force them to return to work the land they had left, and in time it was accepted that the peasant, or serf, belonged to the land, and thus to the landowner. A serf was almost a slave, who could be bought and sold, or even killed by his master.

The northern principality of Muscovy finally broke the Tartar yoke under Prince Ivan III in 1480, and Moscow grew to become the new capital of Russia.

The history of Russia after the Tartar period has been in many ways an attempt to catch up with the rest of Western Europe and to make itself secure against attack from outside.

Peter the Great (1682–1725) was the first Russian tsar to travel

The statue of Peter the Great in Leningrad, the city he built as Russia's "window to Europe."

abroad. He learned shipbuilding in Holland and England, and went home determined to westernize Russia. For most of his reign he was at war and won the Baltic port of Riga from the Swedes. He also founded a new port — his capital, St. Petersburg (now known as Leningrad).

The Russian resistance to Napoleon's attack in 1812 aroused great national patriotism. Moscow was abandoned and set ablaze to cheat the French emperor. The tired French soldiers were frozen in the Russian winter, and then pursued all the way back to Paris.

Liberal Paris and the ideals of the French Revolution of 1789 stirred similar ideas in the Russians. A plot to assassinate the tsar in December 1825 failed. Nicholas I responded

The retreat of the French army from Moscow, 1812.

by passing stricter security laws to control the people. He became even more unpopular when Russia was humiliated by defeat in the Crimean War of 1853–56.

The next tsar, Alexander II, felt that liberal reforms were necessary to avoid the threat of revolution. Laws were passed to end serfdom in 1861, but these laws were so favorable to the landowners that some serfs were worse off than they had been before. Alexander was killed by a terrorist bomb in 1881, and more repression followed.

It was not until 1905 that the peasants achieved anything close to civil liberty. Ten years later came serious military defeats by Germany, in World War I (1914–18). Severe food shortages, strikes and riots forced Tsar Nicholas II to

Above *The last Russian tsar, Nicholas II, and the tsarina, Alexandra.*

Right *A revolutionary poster of Lenin commemorating his death in 1924.*

abdicate in 1917. In November 1917 came the Bolshevik Revolution, led by V.I. Lenin. The tsar and his family were shot in July 1918.

The final victory for the Revolution was not achieved until after three years of bloody civil war, in which 13 million people died. Britain, France, the United States and Japan joined in the opposition to the Bolsheviks.

Lenin, exhausted by his revolutionary struggle, died in 1924. The leadership then fell to Joseph Stalin, who crushed all opposition to his own policies, imprisoned or shot his rivals, and established a personal reign of terror as bad as or worse than that of any previous Tartar ruler or tsar. Yet he also modernized Soviet industry, which saved the country when it was attacked by Nazi Germany in 1941.

More than 20 million Russians died in World War II (1939–45). The Russian winter, however, had a deadly effect on the invading German army, which came within 20 km (12 mi) of Moscow.

Stalin died in 1953. During his leadership, many loyal Russians

disappeared into labor camps and were never seen again. It has taken until the present day for the effects of his regime to start to fade. Seventy years after the Russian Revolution, Mikhail Gorbachev's leadership is encouraging a more openly critical attitude toward social and industrial restructuring. The emphasis is now on a higher standard of living for all of the people of the USSR.

In spite of this somewhat bleak history of hardship and struggle for survival, the effects on the character of the people are

Mikhail Gorbachev became the Russian leader in 1985 determined to encourage "Glasnost." This Russian word means "to be open" or "to make public" and is now used to describe Gorbachev's style of government.

surprisingly positive. The Russians are extremely cheerful, talkative and patient people, who are always prepared to take a long-term view — they do not expect all of their problems to be solved tomorrow, and would rather secure future benefits for their children and grandchildren than immediate advantages for themselves.

Russian food in history

Russian cooking began to develop in the period of Kiev Rus (880–1240) and reached its peak in the reign of Ivan the Terrible (1533–84). During these years, sour-dough rye bread, *blini*, all sorts of *kashas*, cabbage soup and honey drinks became the basis of the Russian diet.

The monks in the monasteries of Kiev Rus were the first people to record the diet and eating habits of the early Russians. At this time, the turnip and the cabbage were staple

A cell in a monastery where the monks of Kiev Rus lived (around A.D. 1200).

foods for the Russian Slavs: a bad turnip harvest was a national disaster as serious as an enemy attack or an outbreak of the plague. Only after 1780 did the turnip lose popularity – in favor of the potato, which was introduced at this time. Cabbage has always been an important vegetable, ever since it was first introduced from the Mediterranean countries.

The black radish and the cucumber are two more vegetables that have been cultivated by the Russians for many centuries and are still as popular as ever.

Apples, pears, plums and cherries have long been used in the preparation of drinks, candy and desserts. Other fruits, such as lemons, oranges, peaches, pomegranates, figs and dates were gradually brought to Russia during the period of Tartar control.

The Tartar contribution to Russian food was both considerable and beneficial. New spices such as ginger, cardamom, cinnamon and saffron began to be used. Dried fruits — apricots, raisins, figs, dates and peaches — were brought in by traveling merchants. The Russians usually rejected the foods of their invaders, but later (when the Tartar lands were part of the Russian Empire) their dishes were adopted and became very popular.

Russians have cultivated cucumbers for many centuries. Pickled cucumbers, like those in the picture, are especially popular.

The earliest way to cook meat was by roasting it over an open fire. In A.D. 964, Prince Sviatoslav (the first Viking ruler of Kiev Rus to be given a Slav name) thinly sliced meat and grilled it over charcoal when he went traveling. But the Russian stoves in the peasant huts favored baking, boiling and stewing for meat and fish.

The actual choice of food depended largely upon what was available within a particular area. In the north it included moose, reindeer and bear meat. There have always been very large areas of forest in Russia, offering a wide variety of game for hunting, as well as mushrooms, nuts and wild berries for gathering. All these made good ingredients for the stewpot, as did the many varieties of fish from the rivers and lakes.

After the sixteenth century, influence from Western Europe played a part with the introduction of lettuce, beans and tomatoes, as well as coffee.

The Russian tsar, Peter the Great, introduced a new stove, having a hot-plate on top for frying, which had not previously been possible. He also made it fashionable for well-to-do families to employ

foreign chefs (preferably French or German) and, as a result, Russian cuisine took a new direction. A French chef created beef *Stroganov* for Count Pavel Stroganov, another chef flattered his master by naming the dish veal *Orlov* after him. Some chefs are remembered by their own names. Salad *Olivier* for example, was created by the owner of Moscow's

Charlotte Russe is a cold dessert that was first created by Antoine Carême when he went to Russia in 1815.

Hermitage restaurant in the 1860s. It inspired a whole series of new salads, of which salad *Stolichnij* is today the best known (see recipe).

The greatest of the French chefs to work in Russia was Antoine Carême, (1784–1833), who came to the court of Alexander I in 1815. Carême had first worked for Charles Maurice de Talleyrand, Napoleon's foreign minister, and in later years worked for Baron Rothschild. He wrote five books on cooking and raised Russian cooking to the standard of European haute cuisine. Probably one of Carême's most famous dishes was *Charlotte Russe*, popular in England, France and Russia.

Salad *Stolichnij*

You will need:
5 or 6 medium sized potatoes
½ lb cooked turkey, chicken, or any other cooked meat
2 eggs, hard boiled
1 medium sized apple
Half a cucumber
1 carrot
A few leaves of white cabbage
½ cup fresh or frozen (cooked) peas
¾ cup of mayonnaise
A few scallions (green onions)
Salt and freshly ground black pepper

What to do:
(1) Remove the meat from the bones and cut into ½-inch cubes. Cut the unpeeled cucumber and cooked potatoes into small chunks. Finely shred the cabbage. Scrub and coarsely grate the carrot, followed by the cored apple. Drain the green peas. Shell the eggs and thinly slice them. (2) Combine all the ingredients in a large mixing bowl, pour over the mayonnaise and season with salt and pepper. Mix well and mound on a serving bowl. (3) Smooth the top of the salad and decorate it with a few chopped scallions, or if you want to make it look like a festive dish, you can decorate it with "mushrooms" made from shelled hard-boiled eggs, topped with half a tomato and a few dots of mayonnaise.

Growing the food

Almost all of European Russia lies in the cold and moderate temperature zone, so its climate is more similar to that of Canada than the United States. It is a climate that has long cold winters and short hot summers, making the average growing season only about four months. This limits the range of crops that can be grown. Even in those areas where the soil is rich, rainfall is irregular; so a winter with little snow, followed by a dry spring and a windy summer, has often resulted in famine. A bad harvest has an immediate effect on meat production as it becomes necessary to slaughter animals that cannot be fed through the long, cold winter months.

The most fertile region of the USSR runs from the Romanian border, north across the Black Sea to the Urals – an area that is more than twice as large as France or Germany. The region is known as the land of the *chernozem*, or black earth.

Cattle on a state farm near Moscow.

Most of the grain produced in the USSR is grown in the *chernozem* areas of the Russian Republic and the Ukraine. (In a good year this amounts to about 170 million tons, almost 80 percent of the country's production.) The grain is mainly wheat and barley, with lesser amounts of oats, rye and corn, some millet, buckwheat, rice and legumes (peas and beans). The best wheat (used for bread flour) comes from the Kazakh Republic, which produces about 10 percent of the

Buildings on a typically large state farm in Kazakhstan.

total USSR grain crop. Grains are also produced in the republics of Byelorussia, Lithuania and Moldavia. The total amount of grain produced meets about 90 percent of the country's requirement – the remainder has to be imported.

After the Revolution, the policy of collectivization (combining the small peasant farms into enormous state farms) caused much distress and opposition among the peasant farmers. At the same time the state policy of rapid industrial growth meant there was a great movement of population away from agriculture into the industrial towns.

Many of the villages were deserted and, over a period of 50 to 60 years, skills in both animal husbandry and crop raising were lost to succeeding generations. Having no hand in farm management or production planning, the agricultural workers had little interest in the results of their work – there was little they could do to improve efficiency or influence policies. The result has been poor performance in agriculture. The workers on the state farms and in factories, and office workers in rural areas were allotted private plots where they could work in their spare time. Much of the produce from the state farms was wasted, spoiled or lost

Individual plots for growing fruit and vegetables can be seen throughout the whole of the USSR.

through sheer inefficiency and lack of interest, while the quality of the peasants' produce showed all the signs of personal care. Today these individual plots produce two-thirds of the output of potatoes and one-third that of vegetables, fruit, eggs, meat and milk. Steps are now being taken to allow more of the planning to be done locally at the state farms and to encourage farm workers by penalizing wastefulness and carelessness and rewarding the results of good work.

Stores and markets

Magazinij (stores)

Most food stores in the Soviet Union are owned by the state, and food prices are centrally controlled. You pay the same price for potatoes, or cheese or chicken in every store. The shopper can concentrate on the quality of the goods, without having to worry about finding the same thing cheaper in another store.

Most Russian families have refrigerators nowadays but deep-freezers are not yet very common, so housewives tend to shop for food every day.

During the last ten years, self-service supermarkets have begun to replace the smaller stores, as they have elsewhere in Europe. For the Russian housewife this has brought a welcome relief from the triple-line system. This system had one line for selecting the goods and getting them priced, another to pay for them and get a receipt, and a third line to exchange the receipt for the

A food store in Leningrad.

actual goods. However, the grandest grocery store in Moscow, which is popularly known as Yeliseyevsky's, still operates the triple-line in its pre-revolutionary imperial halls.

The new supermarkets are called either *Gastronom* or *Produktij*, but both are the same, selling meat, groceries, milk, bread, fruit and vegetables, wine and beer, all at state-regulated prices.

Specialty stores live side-by-side with the supermarkets:

Myaso (meat) is the name of the butcher shop selling mainly beef, pork and offal, but also lamb, chicken and duck, although not sausages. Pigs' feet and cow-heels are in constant demand for making jellied meat dishes.

Dary prirody means "nature's gifts" and is the name given to stores selling dried fruits, berries, wild mushrooms and game. The game includes grouse, partridge and ptarmigan, moose, venison, reindeer and bear meat. These are protected species, hunted only in season by official keepers.

Ovoshi i frukti (vegetables and fruit) sells vegetables such as potatoes, onions, carrots and beets, which are sold all year round, along with *kapusta*, or Russian cabbage. Fresh cucumbers and tomatoes are available in the north in the summer, but are sold pickled in brine all the rest of the year. Summer fruits include grapes and *arbus*, or giant watermelon, from Central Asia and the Black Sea regions.

Kulinariya sells take-out semi-ready foods including risen dough (for pies), marinated meats (for *shashliks*), salads and small pastries. *Okean* (ocean) is the name given to fish stores selling both fresh and frozen fish.

Bulochnaya is a bakery, selling bread, biscuits, pastries and cakes. *Konditerskaya* is a confectioner's shop, selling both candy and rich, elaborately decorated *tortij* – cakes suitable for afternoon tea or at the end of a heavy meal.

The bulochnaya *(bakery) is a very important store because bread is eaten with every meal. There are all kinds of breads available, from dark rye bread to white "French" bread.*

Rijnok (The Market)

Many fresh foods, which are available only seasonally in the state stores, are on sale throughout the year at the farmers' market or *rijnok*. They are produced by peasant farmers, working their own land after a day's work on a state collective farm. Many of them have the food they have grown flown into the cities every day, bringing fresh produce from Georgia, Azerbaijan, Armenia, Uzbekistan and beyond, for sale to the northern industrial workers. The recent advent of cheap air travel allows perishable products to be transported from great distances every day to be sold fresh – at prices that ordinary people are prepared to pay. The markets have been the only officially allowed form of private enterprise in the USSR for a long time. The prices are higher than in the state stores – sometimes five times the price – but the townspeople feel it is worth it for goods that would otherwise not be available. The smells of oriental spices, pickled garlic, freshly cut herbs and flowers fill the market halls. Gold-toothed Georgians compete with high-cheeked Uzbeks in crying out their wares, tempting shoppers with a taste of pomegranate, melon or apricot. Old Russian peasant women, known as *babushkas*, in their shawls, offer honey, *tvorog* (cottage cheese) and *smetana* (sour cream) to sweeten the chill of the Moscow winter.

The marketplaces are permanent indoor structures, provided by the state. Standards of quality and hygiene are controlled by the Soviet Ministry of Food.

An indoor market. Prices are higher than at the stores but the produce is more varied.

The meals

Zavtrak (Breakfast)

Zavtrak is usually a very quick meal during the working week. Everybody in the family is in a hurry: mothers and fathers have to rush to work, and children to school. But while the parents have just an open sandwich with cheese, ham or salami and a cup of coffee, children have a cooked meal, which is usually a boiled egg or an omelette or *kasha. Kasha* can be any cooked grain (cereal), served with milk, sugar and butter. Buckwheat, which is mistakenly called *kasha* in the West, is only one kind of *kasha.*

Obed (Lunch)

Obed is the main meal of the day, eaten between 1 pm and 3 pm. Most of the big factories and offices have their own self-service cafeterias, where the employees can eat their meals at considerably reduced prices. Children have their dinner in the school cafeteria.

Obed starts with a small *zakuska* – salted herring, or some kind of salad – followed by soup. Russian soup is always made from home-made stock, and the quality of the soup depends mainly on what is put into the stock. If it is to be

Kasha, *buckwheat for example, is a very popular breakfast food.*

Shchi *is a favorite Russian soup.*

chicken soup, a whole chicken goes into the pot; if it is a meat soup, then a good chunk of beef will be simmered for two to four hours with some vegetables, and then the stock from this will be enriched with fresh vegetables, dried peas or beans, pasta, rice or barley.

The favorite soups are *shchi* (cabbage soup) and *borsch* (Ukrainian beet soup). They are rich in flavor, quite thick, and are served with a piece of meat in each bowl, almost making a meal in themselves. After the soup comes the main course. Fish is popular and Russians prefer freshwater fish like carp and pike. Tasty meat stews have unusual flavorings of wild mushrooms, pickled cucumbers and *smetana*. *Golubtsy*, cabbage leaves stuffed with meat and rice in a tomato sauce, and *sosiski*, frankfurter-type sausages are also popular main courses, as are *kotleti*, *bitochki* and *tefteli*, which are all dishes based on meatballs. The main course is served with potatoes, pasta or cereal. Some salt-cucumbers will be served too – they are so popular that they accompany nearly every dish as, of course, does bread. Russians eat a lot of bread with their food and it is said that in the old days a peasant would eat as much as a loaf of bread at each meal.

Obed is finished with coffee, tea, *kompot* (stewed fruit) or *kisel*. *Kisel* is fruit juice, thickened with cornstarch. The most popular kind is made from cranberry juice and is a bright purple-red color and slightly tangy in taste.

Uzhin (Supper)

This is the evening meal, when the whole family gathers around the table for the last meal of the day, and to exchange the day's news. Children help their mothers set the table and often wash the dishes after the meal. Soup might be served again, and the main course could be made from vegetables, like potato cakes with mushroom sauce, or *tvorog* (cottage cheese). Tea or a milk drink follows.

Shchi with sauerkraut

You will need:

1½ quarts of good beef stock

1 lb of *sauerkraut* packed in brine, not vinegar. (You can buy it in a delicatessen or supermaket.)

3 tablespoons of butter

1 carrot, coarsely grated

1 onion, peeled and chopped

2 tablespoons of tomato purée

2 bay leaves

5–6 peppercorns

2 cloves of garlic, crushed

2 tablespoons of chopped fresh dill

⅔ cup of sour cream

salt and freshly ground black pepper

What to do:

(1) In a large, covered saucepan, stew the *sauerkraut* with 1 tablespoon of butter over very low heat, for about 1 hour. Meanwhile, melt the rest of the butter in a frying pan, stir in the onions and carrot and cook over gentle heat so the vegetables just soften. Now stir in the tomato pureé and cook for a few minutes longer. (2) When the *sauerkraut* is ready, mix in the fried vegetables, the bay leaves and peppercorns and slowly pour in the stock. Bring to simmering point, cover and cook gently for about 20 minutes. (3) Now turn the heat off, add the crushed garlic and dill to the *shchi*, season with salt and black pepper, and leave in a warm place for the flavors to blend. This blending is very important for the *shchi* and it tastes even better the next day. (4) Add to each plate a slice of boiled meat from the stock (if you made your own) and a tablespoon of sour cream. Serves 6.

Safety note: Be very careful when frying the vegetables — hot oil burns.

Bread

No chapter on Russian meals would be complete without a mention of bread, which has always played a central part in the diet.

Even the Russian word for hospitality is *khlebosol'stvo*, which means "bread and salt." It is an old custom to present a guest with a round loaf of freshly baked bread and a wooden dish of salt. This was a sign of respect and honor. The ceremony is still observed, most regularly at wedding receptions when bread and salt are used to greet the bride and groom when they arrive at the reception.

Russians still prefer to eat dark, heavy rye bread, which comes in many varieties, most of them named after their place of origin. They are all sour-dough breads, though this does not necessarily mean they actually taste sour. The name "sour-dough" refers to the method used to make the bread rise. Instead of using fresh yeast, a piece of dough left over from the last session of bread making is used to make the new dough ferment. The Slavs probably learned this method of bread making from the Greeks, in the days of Kiev Rus, before yeast was discovered. According to the old recipe books, the whole process, from mixing the dough to baking, could take up to five days.

In the bakeries there are always three or four different kinds of rye

Bread that has been baked in a traditional Russian oven, or pech.

bread available. The blackest one is *borodinsky*, a very rich, tasty bread, covered with coriander seeds. *Rizhsky* is much lighter and is flavored with caraway seeds. *Orlovsky* is a "gray" bread, having a higher proportion of wheat flour. These breads were originally from Borodino, Riga and Orel.

For many years white bread was only available from the French bakeries in the cities, but today the demand for it is almost as great as for rye bread. Many different kinds and shapes are available. One kind of roll, the *kalach*, is shaped like a large padlock. It was originally the worker's standard lunch, held by the clasp to keep it clean.

Eating out

Cafés and Snack Bars

For lunches, quick meals and snacks, there are cafés and self-service restaurants offering a selection of dishes or specializing in quick food. The *cheburechnaya* is a type of street café selling *chebureki*, which are Tartar deep-fried mutton pies, flavored with onion, pepper and parsley. (When biting these, be careful not to let the juice run down your sleeve!)

The *pel'mennia* serves a Siberian pasta, slightly similar to Italian ravioli, with a meat filling, and garnished with *smetana* or with butter and vinegar. The *shashlichnaya* is a kebab house offering Caucasian food: lamb and beef kebabs and chicken *tabaka* – a flattened spring chicken, fried in butter and served with garlic sauce.

The *molochnaya* (dairy café) specializes in milk and cheese-based dishes: *sirniki*, fried *tvorog* cakes; *zapekanka*, a cheese pudding

Ice cream can be bought from either an ice cream parlor, or a street seller like this one.

made from *tvorog*, eggs and raisins. All kinds of milk drinks are sold here too.

The *chainaya* is a tea house serving tea and cakes.

The *café morozhennoye* is an ice cream parlor, crowded in both summer and winter. There are also ice cream stands in the streets open all year round. Street kiosks sell meat pies (*pirozhki*), doughnuts (*ponchiki*) and hot coffee.

Restaurants

The Russians have a very definite idea about what a good restaurant should be: it is not just somewhere to eat – it must be capable of providing a full evening's entertainment, with food, drink, a band for dancing and maybe a floor show. The best restaurants, in the large cities, are splendid places, brilliantly decorated and full of activity. Five minutes walk from Red Square, in the center of Moscow, tucked away by the old *Kitaiskaya Stena* (or Chinese Wall), is the Slavyanski Bazar – the most "Russian" of restaurants complete with a *balalaika* band playing a sad, gentle folk song or breathless cossack dances. But a foreigner might be puzzled and perhaps irritated by the slowness of the service, for the Russians do not hurry when they have come for a serious meal – they are there for the whole evening.

The Slavyanski Bazar is famous for its traditional Russian dishes. The meal must start with a selection of *zakuski*. Caviar is served here

The restaurant table is a magnificent sight.

Salad matrioshka.

with *rasstegai* – small pies, filled to bursting with a mixture of fish, onion, parsley and *smetana*; a dish of mushrooms baked in sour cream; the house salad *matrioshka*, with potato, pickled cucumber, eggs and meat and smoked sturgeon with cucumber. Russian black rye bread is served as a matter of course. For Russians, vodka is almost the only possible drink for this occasion, although the menu also includes Georgian and Crimean wines. The soup course might be fish *solyanka* made with sturgeon, salt-cucumber, potatoes, olives and lemon, and to follow for the main course, a very slavonic stew, *goviadina po Russki*. This is a beef stew with carrots, onions, salt-cucumber, mushrooms and puréed tomatoes, baked in individual clay pots. Almost the only possible dessert after such a heavy meal is ice cream. This is a lot of food, but spread over three or four hours and with dancing, it is really surprising how much you can eat! In many of the big cities, there are restaurants for the national cuisine of other Soviet republic. They provide food and entertainment on a similar scale. Three Moscow restaurants, the Aragvi (Georgian), Baku (Azerbaijan) and Uzbekistan, provide a colorful introduction to exotic foods from the Caucasus and Central Asia; they are also three of the best restaurants in town. But it is not only in the center of the big cities that you find restaurants providing this traditional hospitality: it is part of the way of life in the suburbs and lesser towns too.

Regional specialties

The population of the USSR totals more than 260 million, of whom just about one half are actually Russian. There are 40 million Ukrainians and 10 million Byelorussians, who are also East Slavs, having fairly similar cultural and kitchen traditions. The remainder of the population come from completely different cultures: there are about 16 million of Turkic origin (Tartars, Kazakhs and Azers), 6 million Uzbeks (of mixed TurkoIrano-Mongol origin), and 3 million each of Georgians and Armenians

Caviar is the roe from fish of the sturgeon family.

living in the Caucasian republics. On the Baltic coast, the Estonians, Latvians and Lithuanians total about 7 million. The Moldavians, who live close to Romania, claim to be descended from Roman legionnaires. In eastern Siberia, the Chukchi and Evenki have a way of life similar to that of the Inuit (the Eskimos).

Close involvement over many centuries with these other cultural traditions has resulted in many foods' being absorbed permanently into Russian cuisine. This is certainly true of fish dishes such as *sprotij* (smoked sprats) and *salaka* (herring), coming from the Baltic regions, and sturgeon and caviar from the Caspian. *Plov* (pilaf), from the Turks, and *shashlik* (kebabs), from the Caucasus, are also everyday foods for Russians, as are the *saliankas* from Armenia (soupstews of fish or meat). The Tartar Mongols ate a lot of horse meat and drank *koumis* (fermented mare's milk), but these never became popular with the Slavs, although *chebureki* certainly did (see p. 25).

The Russians have a great liking for the spicy cooking of Georgia. There is a mutton soup, *kharcho*, which is flavored with coriander and hot with peppers; chicken *satsivi* (see recipe) and chicken *tabaka*, which seems to be steam-

Chicken *satsivi*

You will need:

A 3½ lb roasting chicken
1½ quarts of water
2 bay leaves
1 onion
½ teaspoon of dried tarragon
2 teaspoons of salt
7 oz of shelled walnuts
3 onions, finely chopped
3 tablespoons of butter
6 cloves of garlic
2 tablespoons of fresh coriander leaves
1 tablespoon of flour
½ teaspoon of ground cloves
½ teaspoon of ground cinnamon
½ teaspoon of mixed dried herbs
¼ teaspoon of cayenne pepper
1 tablespoon of wine vinegar

What to do:

(1) Put the chicken in a saucepan and cover with 1½ quarts water. Add the whole onion, bay leaves, tarragon and salt and bring to a boil. Skim and simmer gently for 40 minutes. When the chicken is ready, remove it from the stock and set it to cool, saving the stock for use later. (2) Crush together the walnuts, garlic, fresh coriander leaves and cayenne pepper, to make a smooth paste. (3) Melt the butter in a heavy saucepan and fry the chopped onions for 5 minutes, sprinkle in the flour and stir well to absorb the juices. Pour in 2 cups of chicken stock, add the walnut paste, vinegar, spices, and dried herbs and simmer slowly for 20 minutes. (4) Cut the chicken into 12 small portions and pour the hot sauce over it. Allow to cool. Serves 6.

Safety note: Be very careful when cutting up the chicken.

rollered, marinated fried chicken. But probably the best Georgian chicken recipe is *chakhokhbilly* – a stew flavored with paprika, coriander, onion, tomatoes and masses of fresh herbs.

Most herbs grow wild in this part of the country, and, with young grape wine and sheep's cheese, have been the main diet of the Georgians for many centuries.

Fresh herbs, such as coriander, parsley, basil (in its deep-purple variety), watercress and tarragon

are served with every meal on a separate platter.

Armenian cooking has some interesting combinations of meat-and-fruit or fish-with-fruit dishes. Apples and quinces stuffed with spicy minced lamb are examples of *dolma* (stuffed vegetables) and are served together with the more familiar stuffed vine leaves and stuffed tomatoes. Baked trout is stuffed with dried apricots, prunes and fresh pomegranates.

The cooking of Azerbaijan has more than a dozen different kinds of *plov: Chikhirtma plov*, with lamb, chicken and chestnuts; *Balic plov*, with fish from the Caspian Sea; and

A shashlik *stand along the roadside. Shashlik originally came from the Caucasus and is very popular with Russians.*

Shirini plov, with fruit, from Persia (Iran). The people of Azerbaijan adopted a refined method for cooking rice from their Persian neighbors. The rice is carefully washed and soaked, to give a light fluffy grain, and is often cooked with *kazmag*, a thin layer of dough

Plov is a favorite dish throughout the USSR and there are various ways of making it. Uzbek plov *is especially popular.*

to prevent the rice from sticking to the bottom of the pan. Saffron from Azerbaijan is used to color and flavor the rice.

Uzbek *plov*

You will need:

1 cup of long grain rice
½ lb of boned lamb, cut into ½-in
    cubes
½ lb of carrots, cut into thin matchsticks
2 medium onions, peeled and sliced into
    half-rings
5 tablespoons of vegetable oil
½ cup of seedless raisins
2 cups of water
½ teaspoon of paprika
¼ teaspoon of cayenne pepper
1 teaspoon of ground cumin
2 teaspoons of salt
(A large cast-iron saucepan with a tightly
    fitting lid)

What to do:

Heat the oil in the saucepan and quickly fry the onions until golden brown. (1) Add the meat and stir-fry together with the onions for about 15 minutes. Finally add the carrots, 1 teaspoon of salt and the spices. Turn the heat down and let it cook very gently for about 30 minutes, stirring from time to time. (2) Throw in the raisins and carefully spoon the rice on top of the meat mixture. (3) Increase the heat to the highest and pour in the water with 1 teaspoon of salt, taking care not to disturb the surface of the rice, and let it boil vigorously till the liquid is absorbed by the rice. Then cover tightly with the lid and turn the heat as low as possible. After 20 minutes, the *plov* should be ready. (4) Mix it gently and serve on warmed plates. Serves 4.

Safety note: Ask an adult to help you to stir-fry the ingredients in the hot oil.

The most popular *plov* is the Uzbek version (see recipe). Here the meat and rice are cooked together, spiced with berberis, saffron, red pepper and *zeera*. It is an ancient dish and the subject of many scholarly books. The Uzbek villages still have competitions to see who can make the best *plov*. (Only men are allowed to enter such competitions.)

The Kazakhs have a specialty called *belyashi*. These are round, open pies, made from chopped mutton and onion, with raised pastry. They are pan-fried (the Tartar *chebureki* are deep-fried) and are best eaten straight from the pan.

In the Slavonic republics, the Ukraine is the homeland of *borsch* (see recipe). There are more than a hundred varieties, some having over twenty ingredients, but all including beets for their deep-red color and sharp flavor. Ukrainian *vareniki* are small pockets of pasta filled with cottage cheese or morello cherries, served with *smetana*. The Ukraine is also famous for its country sausages and freshly salted lard, eaten on black rye bread. We cannot discuss Ukrainian food without mentioning chicken Kiev – which is served in many parts of the world. This famous dish is chicken breasts filled with garlic-butter and deep-fried in egg and breadcrumbs.

Byelorussia (White Russia) is famous for its potato dishes. Potato *zrazy* are cakes made from mashed

Chicken Kiev, chicken breasts stuffed with garlic-butter, appears on menus in restaurants all over the world.

potato, stuffed with chopped beef, fried onions and mushrooms. *Dranki* are thick potato pancakes, served with *smetana*.

The food of the Baltic republics (Latvia, Estonia and Lithuania) is more similar to Scandinavian and German food than to Russian. The delicate Baltic herring is especially delicious in the Estonian salad *rossolye*, which has layers of chopped potatoes, beets and sour apples, under a topping of *smetana* and fresh dill leaves.

Ukrainian *borsch*

You will need:

1½ quarts of good beef stock
1 potato, peeled and diced
3–4 cups of finely shredded cabbage
An 8-oz can or jar of pickled beets
2 tablespoons of butter
1 onion, chopped
1 carrot, coarsely grated
2 tablespoons of tomato purée
1 bay leaf
6 peppercorns
2 tablespoons of cider vinegar
2 cloves of garlic, crushed
1 oz of salt pork or 2 slices of
    unsmoked bacon
2 tablespoons of chopped parsley
salt and freshly ground pepper
⅔ cup of sour cream

What to do:

(1) Pour the stock into a large saucepan, stir in the diced potato and bring to a boil. After 10 minutes, add the shredded cabbage and coarsely grated beets, cover with a lid and allow to simmer over low heat. (2) Meanwhile, melt the butter in a frying pan and soften the onion and carrot in it for about 5 minutes. Stir in the tomato purée and cook for a few minutes longer. (3) Then add these vegetables to the soup, followed by the bay leaf, peppercorns, vinegar and finally the parsley, pounded with the crushed garlic and the bacon. Taste and adjust the seasoning. Put the lid on and continue to cook for a further 20 minutes. (4) Serve with a piece of beef from the stock (if you have made your own) and a spoonful of sour cream in each plate. Serves 6.

Drinks

Chai (Tea)

Russia, Britain and Japan are the world's top tea drinking nations. Tea from China was introduced to the Russian court by the Mongol Khan Altin, as a gift to Tsar Mikhail Romanov in the early seventeenth century. The Russian Boyars were at first suspicious of this bitter drink (as they were of everything foreign, and especially anything coming from the Mongols), but they found it helped them stay awake during long church services and boring political meetings, so it became increasingly popular. From the signing of a trade treaty with China in 1689, tea was brought to Russia by camel caravans – each of two to three hundred camels – taking a whole year for the trip, until the Trans-Siberian Railroad opened in 1880. In 1864 tea growing began in Georgia and Azerbaijan and in south Russia, and it continues today. Tea is also imported now from India and Sri Lanka. The Asian origin of Russian tea drinking is still seen from the continuing use of the *samovar* in making tea. The word *samovar* means "self-boiler." It is a portable water boiler, usually made of brass, using pine cones or charcoal for fuel. It is like an urn with a wide tube down the middle. The tube, when filled with hot charcoal, acts like a chimney causing the fuel to burn red-hot, boiling the water surrounding it. The tea is not made in the *samovar*, but in a small teapot, which is then kept hot on top of the chimney. The brew in the teapot is made as a very strong concentrate, which is diluted with hot water from the *samovar* when served in cups or glasses. It is usually drunk black, sometimes with sugar or lemon, and accompanied as often as possible by a sweet cake, or a small dish of fruit conserve.

Tea being sold from a samovar *to travelers on a train at the beginning of this century.*

35

Soviet Central Asia continues its old tradition of drinking green tea, often spiced with cinnamon, in tea houses known as *chaikhana*.

Coffee

Tsar Peter the Great brought back the fashion of coffee drinking after his tour of England and Holland, in the early eighteenth century. He made it an almost compulsory drink at his court for those who wanted to stay in favor. Later, the Russian soldiers who visited Paris after the defeat of the French emperor, Napoleon, in 1815 grew to like French coffee so much that they left behind the Russian word

This tea house, or chainaya, *sells tea, pies and cakes.*

bistro (fast), which is still used in France to mean a small café where coffee is served quickly.

In Soviet Central Asia, the taste for coffee was introduced by the Turks. It is served thick, black and very sweet, with a glass of water.

Vodka

Vodka is the national drink of Russia. It is produced by distilling a mash made from various grains, usually wheat, barley, or rye, or from potatoes, then repeatedly purified to refine the flavor. Basic

Vodka can be made from either grain or potatoes. It is Russia's national drink.

vodka has no additional flavoring, but the Russians like to flavor it with cranberries, lemon peel, pepper or herbs. They always have something to eat when drinking vodka, such as sour cucumber, pickled mushrooms, black bread or salt herring.

Wine and brandy

The USSR is the world's third largest wine producer, with over three million acres of vineyards in the south of the country. The northern Russians prefer to drink vodka, although they also drink fortified wines, like port, sherry and Madeira, but these are sweetened with added sugar.

The biggest wine producers are the Ukrainian and Moldavian republics, but some of the best wine comes from the Crimea and Georgia. Little of the wine leaves the USSR, except for the red sparkling *Tsimlanskoye Champanskoe* from around Rostov-on-Don, and *Anapa Riesling*, also from the Russian Republic. The best known Georgian wines are *Tsinandali* and *Gourdzhuani* (white), and the heavy red *Mukuzani* and *Saperavi*. *Kinzmarauli* – Stalin's favorite red wine – is rich and full, but too sweet for Western taste. The Moldavian white *Aligote* and *Riesling* are good summer wines, while *Cabernet* and *Romanesti* are traditional reds, which may be laid down to age and kept for special occasions. Other wine producing areas include Azerbaijan (for *Matrasa* and *Sadilly*), Armenia and Uzbekistan. All the wine growing areas also produce high quality brandy: the best probably comes from Georgia and Armenia. Winston Churchill, Britain's leader in World War II, was said to be very fond of Armenian brandy.

Beer

Beer is just as popular in Russia as it is everywhere in Europe. Russian beer is still made by traditional brewing methods, to a very high

standard. *Kvas* is a summer drink made from fermented rye bread. It is like a very weak beer with a slight licorice taste, but is probably no more alcoholic than rootbeer. It is sold on the streets from the *kvas* wagon to quench the thirst of the Muscovites in the very hot Moscow summer.

Other drinks

Fermented milk drinks, similar to buttermilks, are very popular all over the USSR, especially at breakfast time. *Kefir* is cow's milk

Kvas wagons are a common sight during summer in the hot streets of Moscow.

fermented by special yeast to produce a thick refreshing drink. *Prostokvasha* is even thicker than *kefir*. It can be made by adding a little of the whey drained while making cottage cheese to fresh milk and allowing it to ferment in a warm place overnight. Bottled mineral water, from the spas of the Russian Republic and the Caucasus, is also popular for refreshment and because it is believed to be healthy.

Festive foods

All Russian people make the most of any excuse for a celebration, and every event to be celebrated is celebrated in much the same way – by a lengthy feast around a large table, with family, friends and relatives. These meals take place either at home, in a restaurant or in a privately rented room. If they are at home, the women in the family assist each other in preparing the food for two or three days before the party.

The events that are celebrated now include both the traditional feasts of the Russian Orthodox calendar (Easter, Christmas and the start of Lent) and the more recent anniversaries introduced since the Revolution: May Day, The November Holiday and International Women's Day (March 8). To these are added occasions in the individual family – birthdays, weddings, arrivals, departures, reunions, births and deaths. The feasts usually start some time from 2 pm to 5 pm and sometimes they do not finish until after midnight. Throughout a feast, the company sits around the table eating, drinking, talking and making speeches. Continuity in the eating is provided by the *zakuski* – a Russian word that has no direct equivalent in English, although it is sometimes translated as "snacks" or "hors d'oeuvres." *Zakuski* are dishes of food, which are set out on the table from the start of the meal, and which are added to throughout its course. Some examples of *zakuski* are red and black caviar on hard-boiled eggs, jellied sturgeon, smoked sprats (*shprotij*), various salads, such as salad *Stolichnij* or beet salad, *pirozhki* (pies) with meat, cabbage or chopped egg and scallions, pickled mushrooms, smoked and jellied meats, salamis and pâtés.

The meal starts formally when the host raises his glass of vodka, and proposes a toast, welcoming the guests to the celebration. Everyone drinks at the same moment (this is most important in Russia) so the toasts must follow regularly, in a traditional sequence,

Zakuski *are an essential part of any celebration.*

with each guest proposing at least one toast during the evening. Between the toasts, which tend to occur about every ten minutes, everyone eats *zakuski* and talks – or occasionally gets up to dance with a fellow guest. After about two hours of this, the soup (maybe *borsch* or *shchi*) is served, followed by a further hour-or-so of *zakuski*, toasts and talk. Then comes the main course, which might be baked sturgeon, roast beef or lamb, or a regional stew. Once again, this is followed by further talk, toasts and *zakuski*. As the evening goes on,

Beautifully painted eggs could be bought on the streets during the period of Easter in Old Russia.

rich cakes (such as "bird's milk," Kiev's cake, *Podarochny* and Napoleon) or ice cream are served, followed by tea from the *samovar*.

The children are also involved in these family gatherings, but they are allowed to leave the table to play when they have had enough to eat. On New Year's Eve, the table is laid out as elaborately as usual, but the feast starts at midnight. On the last stroke of midnight a bottle of champagne is opened to celebrate the arrival of the New Year, and the feast continues until 4 am or 5 am in the morning.

Paskha (Easter) is by far the most important holiday in the calendar of the Russian Orthodox Church. It is still a time of great feasting and

merrymaking. Special food is prepared during the whole week preceding Easter day. Dozens of hard-boiled eggs are dyed or painted. It is the custom during Easter week to exchange these eggs with friends.

Traditionally, tall, saffron-scented

Traditional cakes are still baked to celebrate Easter.

cakes, often one for each member of the family, are baked and decorated with icing and a very special soft cheese, *paskha*, is taken out of its mold and arranged as the

---

Paskha

You will need:
2 cups of farmer's pot cheese (dry-curd cottage cheese)
½ cup of unsalted butter (softened)
½ to ⅔ cup heavy cream
1 egg, separated
½ cup of sugar
¾ cup of a mixture of almonds, raisins and candied peel

What to do:
Start the preparation at least 24 hours before it is to be eaten. Mix the farmer's cheese with the butter, egg yolk, sugar and cream. Beat it all together to dissolve any lumps. Beat the egg white and gently fold it into the mixture. Chop the almonds and mix them together with the raisins and candied peel into the curd cheese. Line a mold with cheese cloth and pour in the cheese mixture. Put a weight on it and leave it for at least 24 hours in a refrigerator. Next day shake the *paskha* out of the mold onto a pretty serving plate.

Blini *are usually served with caviar and* smetana.

centerpiece of the table. In former years, the food was taken to the church at the midnight mass, to be blessed by the priest. After the service, in the early hours of the morning, the people returned from the church to their Easter breakfast and the feast would start, continuing for nearly a week. People visited each other, exchanging their decorated eggs, kissing each other three times on the cheeks and saying the seasonal greeting "Christ is risen." The table was kept laden with food throughout the whole week.

Maslenitsa, the Russian Pancake Festival, lasts for the whole week preceding the fast of Lent. It used to be a real carnival time, when ice-hills were built for sliding down and young people would race in *troikas* (sleds drawn by three horses) in the countryside. Russian pancakes (*blini*), which are served with hot butter, *smetana*, herring and caviar, are eaten throughout the week. The merchants used to bet who could eat the most and there are tales about some of them even dying from overeating!

Blini

You will need:
1⅔ cups of all-purpose flour
1½ cups of milk (warm)
2 teaspoons of dry yeast
1 egg, separated
2 tablespoons of butter, melted
½ teaspoon of salt
½ teaspoon of sugar

What to do:
Start the preparation at least 3 hours before the meal. (1) Sift the flour into a large bowl. Warm the milk to lukewarm. Dissolve the yeast and sugar in 1 cup of the warm milk. Pour the mixture into the flour and beat it well to dissolve all the lumps. Cover the bowl and leave in a warm place for 1 hour. (2) Now stir the egg yolk, butter and salt together and mix it into the batter. Pour in the rest of the warm milk. Stir until you have a smooth, rather thin batter. Cover the bowl again and leave it to rise once more, for about 2 hours. (3) Beat the egg white until stiff but not dry and, when the batter has risen again, fold the egg white into it. The *blini* should be cooked in a heavy-bottomed frying pan, over medium heat. Rub the pan with cooking oil and pour in about 3 tablespoons of batter. After 2 or 3 minutes holes will appear on the surface. (4) Turn the *blini* and cook on the other side until it is nicely brown.

Safety note: Take special precautions when cooking the *blini*: ask an adult to help you with the first few.

Appendix

The Russian stove

Considering the bitter cold of the Russian winters, it is not surprising to find that the fireplace was an especially important feature in Russian dwellings of every social class. In the thatched wooden cottages of the peasants, the Russian stove, or *pech*, was like a big altar, occupying up to one third of the floor space. It was used for heating, cooking, drying herbs, and finally sleeping – either on top or on a special sleeping ledge. (One popular fairy-tale hero, Emelya, even commands the stove "Off you go, *Pechka*, take me to the tsar's palace," – and it goes so fast that no one can catch up with it.)

The design of the stove, which is still used in many houses, has developed over thousands of years. It has two ovens: one is warm, for slow stewing, and the other is very hot, for baking bread and pies. Built solidly of bricks and mortar, it holds its heat and burns wood slowly and economically. In big houses, stoves were once decorated with beautiful tiles. The construction of the stove accounts for the large number of baked, boiled and stewed dishes found in Russian cuisine.

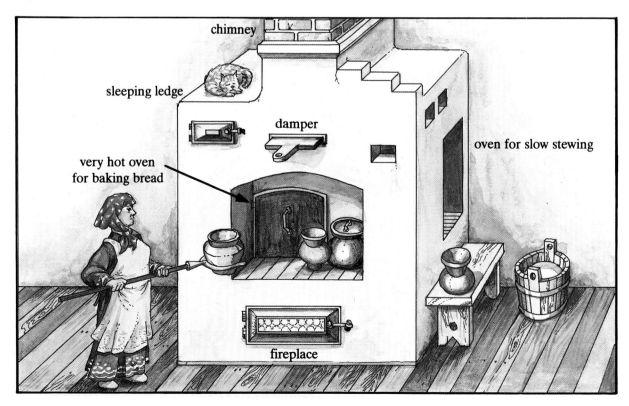

chimney

sleeping ledge

damper

very hot oven for baking bread

oven for slow stewing

fireplace

Note on the Russian alphabet

The Russian (Cyrillic) alphabet has thirty-two characters only six of which have the same sound-values as the English alphabet: they are A, E, K, M, O, and T. Six other characters look the same as in the English alphabet but have different sound values: they are B, C, H, P, Y and X, which have similar sounds to English V, S, N, R, U and Kh (the sound represented by "ch" at the end of the Scottish word "loch" and found in *Chekhov*, *Kazakh* and *Khruschov*).

Some of the remaining Russian characters represent sounds that have no English equivalent and are difficult to describe – the worst being "Ы," which is a deep, almost glottal, throaty "e" sound. We have represented this letter by "ij," as in the words *shprotij* (smoked sprats) and *rijnok* (market).

Glossary

Animal husbandry The science of breeding, rearing and caring for farm animals.

Balalaika A plucked musical instrument, usually having a triangular body and three strings. Used mainly for Russian folk music.

Berberis Little red berries with a sour taste, added to flavor *plov* and drinks.

Boyar A member of the aristocracy in Old Russia, prior to Peter the Great's reign (1682–1725).

Caviar The fresh or salted roe (eggs) of sturgeon.

Cossacks Peasants who lived on communes, especially in the Ukraine, and served as cavalry under the tzars.

Dill A feathery herb, tasting slightly of caraway, especially good with fish dishes, coleslaw and cucumbers.

Genghis Khan Mongol conqueror (c.1162–1227) and founder of the greatest land empire in world history, stretching from Poland to Korea and from Persia to the Arctic. His name was Temojin: Genghis Khan means "Universal Ruler." The brilliant cavalry of the Tartar Mongols was the only army in history to defeat the Russians in winter – which it did by galloping up the frozen rivers.

Gourmet A person having a taste for good food, delicacies and wine.

Haute cuisine Food of the highest professional standards, cooked and presented by chefs.

Labor camp A camp where prisoners were sent, which

involved them in forced manual labor.

Mongol hordes The Tartar Mongols were nomadic peoples who lived in camps. "Horde" is the Mongol word meaning camp and the camp that tyrannized Russia was known as the Golden Horde.

Offal The nutritious insides of an animal such as the heart, liver, kidneys and tongue.

Saffron A spice used for flavoring and coloring festive dishes. One of the most expensive spices, it is obtained from the stigma of a special mauve crocus, which in the USSR grows mostly in Azerbaijan.

Serf An unfree person bound to the land. If the serf's owner sold the land, the serf was passed on to the new landowner.

Smetana Cream that has been allowed to go slightly cheesy by the addition of a special culture. It does not curdle when added to soup and is quite different in flavor and texture from sour cream – it does not have a sour taste.

Steppes Great expanses of grassy, almost treeless, plain (in Eastern Europe and Asia).

Sturgeon A large fish with a row of spines along its body. It is especially valued as a source of caviar.

Tsar The Russian equivalent of "Caesar" or emperor. This title was first used by Ivan III (the Great) who broke the Tartar yoke in 1480.

Zeera A spice similar to black cumin. It is sometimes substituted by cumin in flavoring *plov*.

Further reading

Around the World in Eighty Dishes by Polly and Tasha Van der Linde. Scroll Press.

Christmas Cooking around the World by Susan Purdy. Franklin Watts, 1983.

Cooking of Scandinavia by Dale Brown. Silver, 1968.

Follow the Sun: International Cooking for Young People by Mary Deming and Joyce Haddard. Sun Scope, 1982.

Let's Look up Food from Many Lands by Beverly Birch. Silver, 1985.

Russia in Pictures by the Sterling Publishing Co. Editors. Sterling, 1966.

Russians in America by Nancy Eubank. Lerner Publications, 1979

Soviet Union: Land of Many Peoples by Lane W. Watson. Garrard, 1973.

Take a Trip to Russia by Keith Lye. Franklin Watts, 1982.

Through the Year in Russia by Pamela Barlow. David and Charles, 1981.

Index

Picture Acknowledgments

The publishers would like to thank the following for their permission to reproduce copyright pictures: Anthony Blake 13, 33; Bruce Coleman 28; C M Dixon 15; NOVOSTI 8, 31; Picturepoint 42; Society for Cultural Relations with the USSR 11, 21, 22, 27; Spectrum Colour Library 16, 38; John Massey Stewart 9(left), 19, 20, 30, 35, 37; TASS 17, 24, 26; Topham Picture Library *cover*, 4, 7, 9(right), 10, 12, 18, 25, 39, 40, 41; ZEFA 6, 36. The map on page 5 and illustration on page 44 are by Malcolm Walker. All step-by-step illustrations are by Juliette Nicholson.